Pathways to Devotion VI
By Linda McBurney-Gunhouse

Published by:
Creative Focus Publishing
Winnipeg Beach, Manitoba,
Canada

Cover Artwork by Linda McBurney-Gunhouse
ISBN: 978-1-928071-18-1

Copyright © 2008 by Linda McBurney-Gunhouse
All Rights Reserved.
R3

Published by:
Creative Focus Publishing
Box 704
Winnipeg Beach, Manitoba R0C 3G0
CANADA

Please visit our website:
www.creativefocus.ca

Contact us at:
info@creativefocus.ca

All Scripture is taken from the King James Version of the Bible, unless otherwise stated.

A Note from the Author

Pathways to Devotion VI, is the sixth in a series of devotional books, offering new and insightful inspirational reflections to encourage you as you journey along through life's many interesting pathways. Backed by spiritual themes, you'll find quotes from the Bible in each reflection, designed to uplift, strengthen and create pause for thought.

Many of the reflections are little stories of interesting, insightful and even miraculous things that have happened to me. Other reflections discuss more recent events that also offer inspiring, and hope-filled spiritual applications. Underlying it all is a faith in a loving God who promises He will be with us throughout all the circumstances of life. At the end of each reflection, is a section called Application. Here, you are given a guideline for further Scripture reading, prayer and further reflection. I invite you to use this book as a companion to your Bible and treat it as either a daily devotional book, or use it as a guideline for small Bible study groups. I leave you with one of my favourite passages of Scripture:

Psalm 23:1-3,6

The LORD is my shepherd; I shall not want. He maketh me to lie down in green pastures: he leadeth me beside the still waters. He restoreth my soul: he leadeth me in the paths of righteousness for his name's sake. Surely goodness and mercy shall follow me all the days of my life: and I will dwell in the house of the LORD forever.

Linda McBurney-Gunhouse
Winnipeg Beach, MB
Canada

Contents

Day 1 - Against the Current 1
Day 2 - Being Alone................................... 3
Day 3 - Which Way to Go? 5
Day 4 - Forbidden Knowledge 7
Day 5 - A Rainy Summer 9
Day 6 - A Miraculous Move............................11
Day 7 - A Timely Bug Bite 13
Day 8 - Guided Sight 15
Day 9 - The Great Purge 17
Day 10 - The Truth about Wealth.....................19
Day 11 - Ministry by Faith..........................21
Day 12 - The Power of Repentance....................23
Day 13 - A Forgotten Kingdom 25
Day 14 - About the Cross 27
Day 15 - A Heart Issue 29
Day 16 - Out of Sight...............................31
Day 17 - A Way Out 33
Day 18 - Pool Problems 35
Day 19 - A New View.................................37
Day 20 - Beware the Senses 39
Day 21 - Prepare for Battle 41
Day 22 - A Comforting Shelter 43
Day 23 - Attracted to the Light.....................45
Day 24 - Circle of Intimacy.........................47
Day 25 - What's in a Name?..........................49
Day 26 - Short-change Religion......................51
Day 27 - Summer Olympics............................53
Day 28 - Atmosphere of Praise 55
Day 29 - Rulership 57
Day 30 - So Many Choices 59
An Invitation for Salvation 61
About the Author...................................62
Other Titles.......................................64

This book is dedicated to my readers, who have faithfully provided me with the encouragement and inspiration to continue writing. May God Bless all who continue to read.

Day 1 - <u>Against the Current</u>

Come to Me all you who labor and are heavy laden, and I will give you rest. Matthew 11:28

One summer evening my husband and I were walking along the wooden boardwalk along the beach in the resort town where we have a house. We saw the strangest thing! There was a little white dog in the lake paddling like crazy, but he wasn't moving any closer to shore. His master was on the shore calling him over and over again, not noticing that although the dog was furiously paddling to get to his master, he wasn't moving towards the shore. In fact, it looked like the dog was standing in one spot paddling away. It looked so funny we had to laugh! As we stood and watched, my husband noticed that he was paddling against a current that was slowly moving him away from the shore and he was too small to fight against it. Lake Winnipeg is so large, you can't see an end to it. Being a shallow lake, there is an undertow that you don't always know is there until you go in the water and then try to swim against it. This is what the dog was fighting against. Finally, the owner went in and rescued his little dog. Even while he carried him to shore, the dog kept paddling and flailing his paws in the air, probably traumatized from the difficult and futile attempts to swim to shore. We watched as the owner held his paws and tried to calm him down.

This incident reminded me that sometimes things happen in our life that are much bigger than we can handle, yet still we try and try to overcome the strong tide that continues to work against our efforts to overcome it. Many times, my husband and I have struggled against financial setbacks. It's not just one thing, but many things, like the time we discovered we needed a few major repairs on our house that had to be fixed all at once (plumbing, electrical and water usage) in order for us to be able to use the house at all. We hadn't planned for these extra expenses and couldn't begin to know how to pay for it all. So in times like this, we go to God in prayer and ask Him what it is we need to do and what He wants us to do since our own resources are usually insufficient. Then we need to trust him to provide.

Maybe your issues are not financial, but have to do with your health, your loved ones or relationships in your job, school or church. Health problems and relationships that aren't going well can seem insurmountable and can also take a toll on our mental and emotional well-being. Notice in the opening verse (Matt. 11:28), that Jesus is calling people that are laboring and burdened by their labors. Labor is good, but when we are burdened by our labors, Jesus offers us a better way. It may sound simple for the complex problems we are currently facing, but when we come to Jesus with our burdens, there is a promise that He will give us rest. Rather than focus on our inability to solve our problems, we need to drop them at His feet and receive the rest (and instruction) He freely offers. Once rested, we will know with confidence that God will provide whatever we need because we trust in Him.

Application

Read: Matthew 11:28-30

Pray: Whatever problem you face today, take it to Jesus in prayer and ask Him to give you the rest He has promised.

Reflect: Think about a time or two you have been presented with insurmountable problems. What was the outcome and, looking back, what would you do different the next time?

Day 2 - <u>Being Alone</u>

And when He had sent the crowds away, He went up into a mountain apart to pray. And when evening had come, He was there alone. Matthew 14:23

Have you ever had so many things happen to you, that you just wished you could be alone for awhile and escape from it all? Some people are alone, not because of relationship problems, but simply because they either can't get out, or because they find it difficult finding friends and then maintaining those friendships. Sometimes our friends or ourselves just get too busy to visit regularly. It may surprise you, but really there are many thousands, even millions of people in our world today who find themselves alone, and feeling lonely.

For me, I am somewhat of a workaholic. Give me a task, and if I can, I will attack it with such fervency, I will neglect everything else until the task it finished, no matter how long it takes. In many ways, I am goal-oriented and one-track minded when it comes to completing something once I've actually taken the time to start it. Often, the kind of work I do (writing) requires I be alone. One summer, I felt I should spend more time than usual at our house at the Beach. We had lived there for 12 years on and off, so it really was my home in every sense of the word as far as familiarity goes. During that time, I knew I had to get busy and start going through things that we had accumulated over the years, most of which we no longer needed. This took me a full month to do, and basically this was all I did the entire time I was out there. But one day, the Lord spoke to me that I needed to stop every once in awhile and be with people — old friends, neighbours or even just go uptown and say hello to people I could meet at the post office, the beach or on the street. He showed me that what I was doing was using the task I was doing and the seclusion of the Beach house as a means to avoid people altogether. I realized it is much easier to avoid the commitment that friendships require than it is to nurture and develop meaningful friendships and fellowship. Yet I still needed the people contact, even if only briefly.

At the end of the month, I had planned to be finished going through things and then start on my crafts. But the Lord had other plans. He wanted me back in the city where I would once again be focused to write, and also be in contact with many more people than I was at the Beach. It was a rude awakening and one that shocked me back into realizing I was to be available and supportive to people who needed me, rather than hide away at a beautiful resort doing tasks that could wait for yet another season of my life. Sometimes God will ask us to be alone so that we can complete a task, get some rest, and also because He wants to fellowship with us. Notice in the opening verse (Matt. 14:23) that Jesus knows the balance. At first He was with the crowds, then He sent them away, went to a quiet place and prayed, and then He was alone. May we always check our motives when it comes to being alone, so that we learn the balance of when to be with people and when to be alone.

Application

Read: Matthew 14:14-23

Pray: about finding a balance in your life when it comes to being with people and also when you need to be alone. Pray about all your relationships with others.

Reflect: What are some times you have experienced loneliness? What happened? Write about at least one relationship that needs improving. Do something about it today.

Day 3 - <u>Which Way to Go?</u>

For you shall not go out with haste, nor go by flight; for Jehovah will go before you; and the God of Israel gathers you. Isaiah 52:12

One spring my husband said he had a surprise for me. I couldn't imagine what it was! He did hint that it would get us out, but he didn't say any more. Finally, the parcel arrived and I discovered that it was a GPS, a computerized map system that you put in your car to give you direction. The year before, we had moved into the city and I went into unfamiliar territory and got lost in rush-hour traffic. I kept going down the same streets repeatedly, like someone in a forest might do — after awhile all trees look the same. Finally, in tears, I called my husband on my cell phone and asked him to guide me back to the condo. So it was then that he decided we would need a GPS.

Our first long trip using the GPS was down to the Black Hills in South Dakota which we began at the end of June, wanting to avoid heavy traffic, overbooked hotels, etc. We decided to program it to take us on the fastest route since our time was limited (only 5 ½ days, and 2 of those days for travel). We could have programmed it to take us on the shortest route, but we thought we might do this for the trip home. We had never driven through the center of North Dakota before, and had little idea what to expect. Rather than towns and people, we drove mile after mile in what seemed like a prairie wilderness. We saw groups of horses, cows, one or two lakes and the rest was rolling hills, grass and desolation. For the most part, we saw no people and no farms or houses, not even a road beyond the fenced fields to indicate people lived anywhere near — it appeared as no civilization! But this was the fastest route the GPS could find, since there would be no stop signs, traffic lights or even traffic! On our trip back, we decided to over-ride the GPS and pick a more scenic route with towns and villages, and of course we stayed on the Interstate highways.

In many ways, the GPS reminds me of the important roadmaps of life we choose. Similar to many younger people today, when I was in my early 20s, I had no idea where I was going in life. I had big dreams and plans, but rarely had the money or wherewithal to pursue any of them. Being a Christian, I was on the narrow path that Jesus talks about (see Matthew 7:13), but many times I was tempted to take a shorter, easier and faster route to my dreams. Yet God had me wait. Eventually, I did make a decision to go to university and get both my BA and BEd. Years later I pursued the art world — photography, painting and sewing. Added to this, I had to wait a long time for the fulfillment of my biggest heart's desire — a perfect husband. Out of my impatience, I could have married a few times before the right one came along, and this would have shortened my wait considerably. But I wouldn't have experienced the love, joy and purpose I do now with the man God chose for me. Like the GPS that may show you the fastest route, but not always the best one, so is any other way through life that God has not led you to. His way may take some time, but it will be the best route available, best, because He has promised to go before us and make our way clear.

Application

Read: Matthew 7:12-14

Pray: Ask God to reveal any areas in your life where you need His direction. Pray for guidance in all that you do.

Reflect: What is the best guidance you ever received when you wondered which way to go? Write about it and share it with someone today.

Day 4 - <u>Forbidden Knowledge</u>

And Jehovah God commanded the man, saying, You may freely eat of every tree in the garden, but you shall not eat of the tree of knowledge of good and evil. For in the day that you eat of it you shall surely die. Genesis 2:16-17

One day I was reading the above verses and it occurred to me that the word "knowledge" and "die" appear in the same verse. There's another word used that, strangely, doesn't seem to fit and that is the word "freely." So like a puzzle, I wanted to try to make some sense of the verses keeping in mind these three words. God's command may at first glance seem simple enough, but when we look at it more closely, it is actually very profound. First, God gave Adam complete freedom to enjoy from whatever tree he desired and probably eat to his heart's content. But as soon as God pointed out the tree of knowledge of good and evil, He warned Adam against it. Unlike all the other trees that brought forth life, this tree in particular would bring forth death.

In thinking about knowledge, we know that man's reasoning is what sets him apart from the common animal. It is man's ability to reason that enables him to be a completely independent creation, unlike anything else God ever created. And if we read earlier verses in Genesis, the Bible says that we are created in the image of God. If we think of these two things, man's reasoning and also being created in the image of God, as two separate and distinct things, life will not make any sense at all. After all, why would God create man in His own image, give him the ability to reason and then punish him for using that ability?

But I believe that since we are created in God's image, even though we are given free choice and independence, our reasoning must also line up with what God intended in the

Day 4

first place. In my own life, I have learned the kind of thoughts that line up with what God would want me to think, and the other negative thoughts that most likely stem from the tree of knowledge that was forbidden in the Garden of Eden. One of the things I have learned is that thoughts from God are uplifting, encouraging and bring life. Thoughts that are not from God are negative, produce fear and worry, and therefore bring death. Negative thoughts close us in and imprison us, but good thoughts enlarge us and set us free.

We don't think of fear and worry bringing death, but with fear and worry comes a burden and a weight. And since they are not from God, they cannot bring life. Only God can bring about a life change when it comes to our heart, mind and soul. If you really think of it, God imparted a tremendous gift to Adam when He warned him not to eat of the tree of knowledge of good and evil. Adam didn't need to know the dichotomy of good and evil. He was free to enjoy only the good, which God had provided in abundance. Do we sometimes stray from the good thoughts and good things God has abundantly provided for us? We may let our eyes wander and want things we cannot have, but be assured, if God has not freely given it to us, then surely it is not something we need, or that will truly benefit us in the end.

Application

Read: Genesis 2:16-17; 3

Pray: **for God to help you think the kind of thoughts that are from Him, and to discern when your thinking is not from Him.**

Reflect: **Write about what is good knowledge and what is bad knowledge. Write out a plan to think only good thoughts.**

Day 5 - A Rainy Summer

He who gathers in summer is a wise son; but he who sleeps in harvest is a son who causes shame. Proverbs 10:5

Because we live in a colder northern climate, each winter I start to dream about summer and the possibilities of enjoying the many wonderful things to do outdoors. For many years, living in a resort town with a huge lake just down the street, I became accustomed to life at the Beach — this meant swimming, cycling, lots of walking, meeting neighbours on the pier, and later, enjoying free music concerts in the downtown park every weekend all summer long. Summers are always a busy time for us as well, since there is much upkeep in owning an older house. Not only do we care for the lawn and water the plants, but usually we undertake at least one major project a year to help maintain the house. Yet, still we look forward to being outside, even if it means manual labour.

One year our spring arrived late, and then for most of the later spring months, it was cooler and rained a lot. But we thought it would go away and we'd still have a nice hot summer. In late June we went for a holiday to the mid United States, South Dakota. The last time I had been there (Black Hills), was with my parents several years earlier and it was 106 F and my dad's car had no air conditioning. So this time, I thought it would also be hot like it was then. Still, I thought we should pack at least one pair of long pants and one long-sleeved shirt each. It's a good thing we did, because our whole trip was in the mid 60s and even cooler in the hills at night. Even here, we experienced cloudy days and rain. Watching the weather channels, I noticed that it was raining in parts all over North America, which is unusual, since usually it might be only one area at a time.

Many people complained about the rain and cooler weather spoiling the summer because it was difficult to plan

Day 5

anything or even to get any outside work done. Yet, I remembered that early in the spring, because we hadn't had a lot of snow as in other years, that people were concerned about a drought and that this would affect the cost of groceries. In fact, the price of bread rose considerably and in the small town where my sister lives, the cost of groceries did go up. So even though we didn't like to see so much rain, still, rain caused most farmers to have a bumper crop, so that people could be fed and the price of bread, at least, would still be inexpensive to buy.

Also that summer, we had to forego many outdoor activities that we would normally have enjoyed — swimming, gardening and even camping (and not just because of inclement weather). God had other plans for us. He needed us to complete other tasks that were long overdo, like cleaning out our house, sheds and things we had accumulated all the years we had lived at the Beach. He wanted us reading and focusing on His Word, not just on the outdoor activities that would keep us so busy. Sometimes, without even realizing it, we hold to our traditional agendas and are disappointed when things turn out differently. Yet, no matter what the season, or what the weather holds, we must find out God's agenda, for He knows what lay ahead and what we need to do to get there.

Application

<u>Read</u>: Proverbs 6:6-11

<u>Pray</u>: Ask God what His plans are for you and do what He asks even it goes against your original plans.

<u>Reflect</u>: Think of a time your plans changed because of inclement weather. What happened and what did you learn from it?

Day 6 - <u>A Miraculous Move</u>

***The steps of a good man are ordered by the LORD:
and he delighteth in his way. Psalm 37:23***

My mother has lived in a small town in Manitoba for most of her adult years, and loved being there. She has many friends who have been especially dear to her through the years, and especially after my father passed away. Yet, three of her children live in the city about a three to four hour drive away. This can seem far enough, especially in the winter when weather is unpredictable, highways can be slippery or snow-covered, and even close down. Although she made many trips into the city a few times a year to stay for extended periods of time, still, she found going back more difficult each time. She was really missing her children even though she enjoyed all of her many friendships.

After some discussion, and prayerful consideration, she started to think that she would like to live in the city to be closer to her children. But since she has a beautiful cat that she loves and is part of her family, finding an apartment that accepts pets can be a very challenging search, not to mention almost impossible. So we started to search for a seniors complex that would accept pets. My husband and I had moved a year earlier to a condo and just down the street was a seniors complex. I went to inquire to see if there were any suites available and if they would take pets or not. They said they didn't, but were building another seniors residence in another part of the city that would likely accept pets. But it wouldn't be built for another year. They sent me the information which needed to be filled out and returned, and I sent it to my mother.

Meanwhile, over the months, the paperwork became mislaid and we thought for sure that since it hadn't been filled out and sent back, the suites would likely now be gone. We would have to keep searching for a suitable apartment

Day 6

that would accept pets. The next July, my sister made a trip to see my mom, stayed a few days and then brought her to our place in the city. We were going to the Beach the next morning to spend a week or so there so that my mom could have a holiday and be with us. The next morning, just before heading out to the Beach, the phone rang. It was the girl from the management company for the senior residence telling us that the new building was well underway and they were showing display suites. She asked if we wanted to see them. Within the hour we arrived to see the new suites. Out of well over 100 suites, only 24 were set aside for people with pets and they were going fast! So my mother applied for one and was immediately accepted. What a beautiful building complex, in a nice area, with a reasonable price and she could bring her beloved cat.

Was this a coincidence? We knew it couldn't be, because the timing of the phone call was between travel trips (one for her to get to the city and the other out to the Beach). The rest of my family was able to see the suite before they left for holidays, and also agreed that it was the right place for her. The price was right and the place is brand new! Even the date to move in was extended to give her time to get ready for the move. Everything worked out, providing a miracle for my mother to move, even being able to bring the cat that she loves.

Application

Read: Romans 8:28-32

Pray: about any decision in your life that you find difficult. Ask God to give you peace and patience regarding the answer.

Reflect: Describe a miracle God provided for you. Share it today with someone who needs a miracle.

Day 7 - <u>A Timely Bug Bite</u>

For as the heavens are higher than the earth, so are My ways higher than your ways, and My thoughts than your thoughts. Isaiah 55:9

Has God ever allowed something unexpected to happen to you to get your undivided attention? There was a time after we moved from the Beach to the city, that I really longed to go back to the Beach for the entire summer. I tried everything to make this happen. After a late start to the summer, and working hard during the entire month of July, in the Farmers Market and also going through things, I wanted to take the month of August off. I just wanted to relax in the privacy of our fenced in back yard, enjoy on occasional dip in the pool, and maybe get to the writing I had put off for a couple of months. To me, it was going to be my reward for waiting so long for summer to arrive, and also for all the hard work I had done before.

But one by one, God closed that door. In one day, we discovered that we would have no water (except when we hooked into the kind neighbour's water supply), then a couple of days later, discovered that we had an electrical short under the house and also a pipe that was cracked under the house. Likely the pipe froze during the winter, or perhaps just wore out. The week following, I was going to go out to the Beach for the day and bring things in from the house and also drop off the keys to the house so the electrician and plumber could get in. I had packed up the car, and forgot the GPS, so I started back towards the condo, and suddenly felt a sharp pain on the sole of my right foot. I looked down and a large bug flew away from that area. I had been bitten! I immediately put something on it, then realized I couldn't put pressure on my foot. So how could I drive?

My husband wasn't available because he was with his sick father who needed someone to be there in case he needed something. What was God trying to tell me? Earlier that morning after I prayed, I distinctly remember Him asking me to really focus on my writing projects and get them done (one of them this book). I thought He meant over time, that at least I would have this day to go out to the Beach, enjoy a relaxing drive in the country, and then maybe do some writing later in the evening or the next day. But I knew that He wanted me to get to the writing immediately — there was no time to waste. I struggled with this, since I often don't take my writing and the potential good it can do, as seriously as I should. I think of it more as an enjoyable hobby than an actual career or calling. But God sees things differently. So I resumed the writing without hesitation.

Although I didn't understand the urgency of the request, the thought crossed my mind that there was a good unknown reason for me NOT to go to the Beach as planned. Perhaps it prevented a greater disaster, or maybe my husband would need me when he got home from his dad's place. Maybe there is someone who urgently needs my prayers and these books to read. Or maybe Jesus is coming back much sooner than we think. I don't know, but I trust God's direction and His timing. I know that He is always looking out for our best interests and He never asks us to do something without a purpose (see Eccl. 3:1). May we be open to not only listen, but to do what He says without hesitation.

Application

Read: Isaiah 55:6-11

Pray: Ask God to help you do what He's been impressing you to do.

Reflect: Has God ever stopped you in your tracks and changed your plans? What happened? Share your story with a friend.

Day 8 - <u>Guided Sight</u>

Now faith is the substance of things hoped for, the evidence of things not seen. Hebrews 11:1

Most people have at least one medical problem that might be considered less than ideal. For me it seems to be dental. For others it is joint pain, and still others it might be vision. Vision is one area where I have been blessed, and have never been required to get prescription lenses in order to see properly. I am so thankful for being able to see long distances and for the clarity of vision to do the many things I need to do each day.

But one year, the particular optometrist I visited, suggested I get progressive lenses — a fancy lens that is mostly for reading, but also provides vision for distance and arms-length vision. He said they would be more convenient than taking off and putting on reading glasses all the time. I could wear them all the time. So I was kind of excited about this. I ordered the glasses, but when I got them, I couldn't see clearly out of the sides of my eyes — everything went blurry. If I wanted to see sideways, rather than move my eyes I had to move my whole head. There was only one small area of vision I could actually see with. I tried and tried to get used to them, but ended up having eye fatigue, since my eyes were not trained to focus on such a small area. If I was walking on an uneven surface, I would have to take my husband's arm. Or if I was walking up or down a flight of stairs, I had to either take the glasses off or hold onto the guard railing if there was one. Worried and discouraged, I returned them for a full refund, and went back to using my reading glasses only when needed.

As I thought about it, I thought how much, in a spiritual sense, we rely on our natural senses. I was relying on the glasses to help me see better and get somewhere, but they failed to do as I thought they would. This is also what

Day 8

happens when we rely too much on our natural senses. Many people struggle with the whole idea of faith and trusting our lives with a God we cannot see. But nowhere does life get more exciting than when we start to take steps of faith. Soon we see answers to our prayers of faith and in time, we start clearly "seeing" through eyes of understanding. People talk about "blind faith" and believe that if something doesn't make sense, then why do such a thing? But this is the natural senses getting in the way, once again, trying to prevent all the wonderful things God has in store for us when we believe. It is only by acting on our faith that our vision becomes clearer.

How do we obtain faith? Scripture says that Jesus is the Author (originator) and Finisher (perfecter) of our faith (see Heb. 12:2). The faith is already there, we just need to plug into it. The more we read Scripture, the more we "see" Who God is, and what He wants to do in our lives. Many times He will lead us to places we couldn't even dream of. But will this happen with a faulty pair of glasses? Not likely, for if all we do is rely on our limited natural senses, we will fail to see the greater vision that God has in store. We will stumble through life missing many wonderful sights that can only be seen by faith. So we begin by opening our Bible and asking God to reveal Himself and His will through His Word. Then when He wants to take us somewhere, we gladly and willingly follow, trusting implicitly in His loving leadership.

Application

Read: Romans 10:9-17

Pray: for God to help you faithfully read His Word and then follow where He leads.

Reflect: What is the greatest thing God has ever shown you? Write about it and share your experience with a friend.

Day 9 - <u>The Great Purge</u>

For what shall it profit a man if he shall gain the whole world and lose his own soul? Mark 8:36

In a recent book I wrote about marriage, entitled, *The Journey of Oneness*, I discuss that there was one area in our marriage that brought us untold stress. We had accumulated too many things and failed to get rid of things along the way. We have a garage-size shed on our property at the Beach. This was filled to capacity with everything you can imagine — my old arts and education binders from university days, sporting gear, several Christmas bins, my framed paintings and supplies, garden paraphernalia, smaller appliances, wardrobes, bedding and so on. Every time we walked into the shed, it resulted in either laughter, tears, or an inevitable argument. We couldn't seem to find things and didn't even know any more what we were storing. I found it funny that every time I needed to find something (like my box of shrink-wrap watercolor paintings), that it would be hidden in the farthest corner of the shed and I would have to move several heavy bins out of the way in order to get to it. Many times my husband would do this for me, but many times he was away at work, so I would be faced with the daunting task.

What happens when we have too much stuff that we can't seem to part with? We begin storing them. And this takes up space, time and money to buy the things and then to buy something to store them in. Some people, rather than buy bigger bins, buy a bigger house! In fact I heard somewhere that there were people doing just that since they had so much stuff and just kept buying more, not even using the things they were buying. How easy it is when we're shopping to see a sale and believe we "must have it" right away. I had done this many times, and in the area of electronics, so has my husband. So one summer, I knew it was time to clean out the house, the big shed and also one of the smaller sheds.

Day 9

What a big job! We wondered if we should have a huge garage sale and prayed about it. I received an interesting answer: "If you have a garage sale, that (the money) is all you'll get. If you give it away, you will be investing it for a future time." So we opted to give it all away, including furniture we no longer used.

I can't begin to tell you all the good that has come from doing this. Just going through it helped me find things. It also brought closure to my past. It left me with a feeling of freedom from having to worry about what to do with it, and it also curbed my tendency to shop without thinking. I was thrilled that it was going to a good cause or two, and relieved that now there was room to move around in the shed and perhaps now my husband could even do some woodworking or other projects in there. I wouldn't miss any of it and would forget that I ever even had it. I realized also that I didn't need any of that stuff and I can't take any of it with me from this life to the next. Really, all anyone might need in this life is food, clothing and if you live in a cold climate, a warm place to live. May we be always mindful to be free from the things we accumulate and store, and instead store up our riches in heaven.

Application

Read: Mark 8:34-37

Pray: ask God to help you uncover any area of your life that needs to be purged, and then ask Him to help you do it.

Reflect: Is there any area in your life that you need to purge? Identify it and then start doing something to begin purging it from your life today.

Day 10 - <u>The Truth about Wealth</u>

The rich man's wealth is his strong city, and as a high wall in his own mind. Proverbs 18:11

As an enjoyable past-time, my husband and I like to drive around the city or nearby small towns to see how other people live. It gives us lots of ideas and many times we pray for the people living in the houses. One Sunday afternoon, we thought we'd drive to an area north of the city that we'd only heard about, but had never seen. It was still under construction as large, beautiful homes were still being built. As we drove down the streets we admired the large stately homes with double French doors, gleaming large windows and perfectly manicured lawns. Some of the homes were situated on a man-made lake with lit balconies and decks overlooking the water. Other homes had expensive brick work on the front.

Even though it was a beautiful summer evening, we noticed the strangest thing — it was so quiet you could hear a pin drop. No one was around! Either they were tucked away inside and their cars were parked in their elaborate garages, or they were away on a summer holiday. I even wondered if people were working overtime at their jobs to help pay for their extravagant lifestyle. We couldn't begin to imagine how anyone could afford to build such a house and then be able to maintain the mortgage, heating bills and other expenses that such a large home would require. Then there would be the housekeeping and grounds-keeping!

Although we sometimes wish we could buy such a house, since we have only lived in smaller quarters, my husband remarked that if we ever did move to such an area, the first thing we would try to do is get people to come outside of their homes and start mingling with their neighbours. What good is all the wealth in the world, if you have no one to fellowship with? All it amounts to is an empty life, loneliness and perhaps even a fear of people breaking in to steal. Also, it is common for some wealthy people to worry about losing their wealth due to bad investments or other shady dealings.

Many times we may look at how good we think that someone else has it and then feel jealous that we don't have as much. But clearly, wealth comes with a price. If we are wealthy and trust in the money to buy us everything we could ever possibly hope for, we will become a slave to our own riches. We will fear losing it and then we will have nothing. But a life lived with the purest pleasure in the simplest things, such as having a really good family and good friends, is the richest life of all. When I think back on my best memories, they always go back to the good times I had with my family and friends. I also think of the many times I spent in prayer, in reading the Word and in writing these books. These have been the most precious times of all and I wouldn't trade them for all the money in the world. For these have been times spent with Jesus, the One who owns it all, and the One Who knows me and loves me, and continues to provide in abundance for all my needs, fulfilling all my hopes and dreams. God may provide us with the riches of this world, but they were never meant to do anything more than enable us to love and serve Him more, and also attempt to enrich the lives of many others.

Application

Read: 1 Timothy 6:17-19

Pray: Ask God to fill you with a contentment regarding your present lifestyle. Pray for those that are rich and need a Savior.

Reflect: What is your association with wealth? If you are or were wealthy, what would you do to help others for the sake of God's Kingdom?

Day 11 - Ministry by Faith

He therefore that ministereth to you the Spirit, and worketh miracles among you, doeth he it by the works of the law, or by the hearing of faith?
Galatians 3:5

One particularly difficult time when there were many demands on my husband and I, I wondered how we could ever meet the expectations that were beginning to overwhelm us. When loved ones are ill or need a lot of care, it can take a toll on the health and well-being of those trying to help. This, in addition to our jobs and many other demands that needed our immediate attention created a great deal of stress in our lives. Things were breaking down in our house as well, and financially, we were stretched to the limit. Under duress, my husband began battling with his own health issues and then I began to suffer with lack of sleep from all the stress I was feeling. We felt vulnerable and run-down.

When tough times like this hit us, I like to go to the Word of God to find solace, comfort and guidance. This time, the Lord directed me to Galatians 3. The above verse particularly jumped out at me. The gist of Galatians is about freedom from the law and the way it binds us. As I thought about how we were being stretched and pulled and probably doing far more than we really should have, verse 5 began to make sense to me. Were we ministering to others by faith, or were we doing all these things on our own steam, and by our own limited efforts (works of the law)? Many years ago, I came to understand that one of the reasons faith is so crucial to every believer, is that it means we now include God in all of our affairs. When we invite God into our daily lives and in to every situation, He gives us direction to know which tasks to undertake in the first place, peace when we do these tasks, and then strength to do them to completion.

Day 11

When we leave God out of things, we soon run out of strength, patience, money, health, and more.

This is not to be confused with the trying of our faith or with trials that are God-ordained for God's ultimate purposes. Sometimes God allows many things to happen to us like they happened to Job. But Job was not in a ministry position, rather, he was being tested to see if he would still trust in God in spite of all the trials. Also, we must be careful to discern that when we are asked to do or be something that seems beyond what we are able, and we have no peace about it, that it is something that God wants us to walk through. Many times, we can feel pressured by others to do or be something, but clearly God says "no." In everything God calls us to do, there should be a sense of freedom attached to it (see Gal. 5:6-10). Sometimes we simply have to say "no" to people who expect us to do more than we are able or should be doing. Perhaps God has called us to do something entirely different than what others think we should be doing.

So when we find ourselves stretched to the limit and overwhelmed by the many duties that are expected of us, we need to discover if God has actually called us to do these things. Because if He hasn't, then we are trying to minster in our own strength, and not by faith, which will bring God into the situation and all the blessings that are promised when we live by faith (see Gal. 3:8-9).

Application

Read: Galatians 3

Pray: Ask God to help you discern the tasks He wants you to do. Pray about it until you have a definite answer.

Reflect: Write about your own personal experience in ministering by faith. If you have not ministered this way before, pray about it, and then begin today.

Day 12 - <u>The Power of Repentance</u>

Bring forth therefore fruits worthy of repentance;
Matthew 3:8

Recently, I was listening to a guest on a Christian TV program talk about his addiction to pornography and how it was messing up his life. He knew he had a problem and sincerely wanted to be free of this, yet on his own, he couldn't seem to overcome it. He shared that he was delivered only after he admitted his great need of God's help. If you think of it, any addiction, whether it's pornography, alcohol, drugs, gambling or anything else, requires the same kind of admittance.

In some ways, the word "repentance" has been misrepresented to mean something negative. We are sinners in need of being made right. This is a fact of who we are since Adam's fall (see Romans). Yet, the fact that God even allows us the option to repent and be made righteous in Christ, is a great gift in itself. Millions of people can attest the indescribable freedom they have received when they repented. Without God, people think that if they just have enough knowledge, they will be free. So the man who struggled with his addiction to pornography could read as much as he could about overcoming pornography, but still he would not be free. Why? It's like reading about electricity, but if you don't have a lamp and a power outlet, you will still be in the dark. Knowledge does not give us power, only God does.

Repentance does not mean we will never be tempted again. We must always be aware of our need of Jesus, and especially since we can also be attacked by the enemy, Satan, and think that there is no way to overcome our problem because it is part of who we are. Many years ago, I struggled with an anxiety disorder. I went for counseling, I read every book on the subject I could find, I listened to

Day 12

tapes, and I tried to do things I enjoyed to help me relax. I tried everything the books and counselors suggested. Yet, still, I kept having anxiety attacks. I thought if I could just find the source from some part of my past, that knowing this would set me free. But even after I discovered the triggers that would set off an unexpected anxiety attack, I still was not free. Knowledge did nothing to help me, but only seemed to exacerbate the problem. For one thing, I started to believe that anxiety was a generational problem and that I would always be prone to anxiety and depression. How hopeless I felt. But one day, things did change. I discovered that it wasn't generational, but that my thoughts were being subtly invaded by an insidious and evil presence — Satan and his spirit of fear. When I started quoting Scripture to him, he soon went away and the negative thoughts went with him. The truth of God's Word had set me free, not the knowledge from the books and tapes.

In the opening verse, repentance is used with the word "fruits." True repentance brings good fruits. No repentance brings death. When we admit a constant need of God, we are set free from the sins that try to drag us down and enslave us. We receive a new kind of power that no amount of knowledge could ever give us (see John 1:12 KJV). To not repent means we will remain powerless. So we need to continue to humbly turn to Him to meet all of our needs, then we will know His power.

Application

Read: Ephesians 1

Pray: Ask God to search your heart for any area where you need to repent, then do so.

Reflect: Write about a time you repented and received freedom and power. Share your experience with someone today.

Day 13 - A Forgotten Kingdom

For it came to pass, when Solomon was old, that his wives turned away his heart after other gods: and his heart was not perfect with the LORD his God, as was the heart of David his father. 1 Kings 11:4

The account of King Solomon is a fascinating one. He began humble and asked God for wisdom to rule God's people. So God granted him not only wisdom, stature and honor, but because he didn't ask for power, wealth and a long life, God granted him all of that as well (see I Kings 3:5-13). But something happened to Solomon amidst the great blessings God had bestowed on him — he had a weakness for foreign women who worshiped other gods. Solomon had married many women and they would be his downfall. His father David, too, had sinned against God when he took another man's wife for his own. But there was a big difference between David and his son Solomon. David repented and his heart remained true to God. But Solomon's heart was turned away from God, and he refused to repent. So God stripped him of his kingdom.

Recently, I watched a documentary about the temple of Solomon. Only one part of it is left standing. A team of archeologists were going through the rubble of what was left of what used to be a glorious temple built to glorify God. Basically, there was nothing left, not one artifact, not one treasure. King Solomon lost it all. I was particularly interested because of the research I had done on the journey of the children of Israel to the Promised land. Here, too, idolatry surfaced and many of them died without ever reaching the Promised land. Shunning idolatry is the first commandment (Exodus 20:3-6), and is the most elaborated on. God wanted a people exclusively for His own and will never share His glory with another god.

Day 13

I think of our modern day world and although the kingdoms of the world may look different, men's hearts are made of the same stuff. How quickly we can turn our hearts away from God when we are blessed and everything is prospering. When we begin to take pride in our position, whether we are rich or poor, our hearts will be turned away from the God who loves us and prospered us in the first place. Through the ages, we see a trend in revival and notice that when times are hard, people recognize their need for God. When there are wars, famine or natural catastrophe's, people are afraid and some will cry out to God, and often they will turn their hearts towards Him. It is often in these difficult times, that we see how shallow and meaningless wealth, power and position really are when they are not used to glorify God and help others. We may have everything we could want in this life, but when we have lost favor with God, we really end up with nothing in the end. We have lost it all. This is not to say God does not want us to prosper, but it does mean that we must be careful to remain true to our one True God, who never leaves us or forsakes us, in spite of our sins. Do we seek our own glory in this life, or do we choose to live humbly before our God? For this is where the true riches lie.

Application

Read: 1 Kings 11

Pray: Ask God to reveal anything in your heart that is not honoring to Him. Ask Him to remove it.

Reflect: Is there anything in your life that you might love more than God? Write about it and then resolve to turn it over to God today.

Day 14 - <u>About the Cross</u>

For the preaching of the cross is to them that perish foolishness; but unto us which are saved it is the power of God. 1 Corinthians 1:18

Earlier in this book we discuss the power of repentance. Humility is what brings us to repentance and the cross is where we find freedom from our old life that has enslaved us. When I was younger, I heard many sermons about salvation and how to be saved. But for many years, I didn't understand how to continue to live the Christian life after I was saved. So I struggled to make my salvation "stick" to keep me from sinning and living an ungodly life. But try as I may, I kept failing, or backsliding, as the term was called then. This created a struggle that stayed with me for many years. I wondered how I could change things so that God would be pleased with me. I had no assurance of my salvation and after living in the world doing what unsaved people might do (drinking, drugs, partying and so on), I found myself more and more entrenched in ungodly thinking and living.

But one day, things started to change. I came face to face with death. Only 15 years old, I was involved in a serious car accident that I probably shouldn't have survived from. I was so afraid after this, that it changed my thinking about my own mortality and the reality of life after death. Yet still the accident didn't change my heart. Pretty soon I was back into doing worldly things, living with more fear than I could handle. The fear, the drugs and the sinful life I was living eventually led me to have a nervous breakdown. Truly, fear cannot save a person, neither can performing all the good works we can think of. A person's heart has to be changed. But I didn't know any of this, so I felt that my situation was hopeless.

In my late teens, my loving parents sent me to a Bible school in Saskatchewan. Here things started gradually

Day 14

changing. Not only was I learning proper Biblical teaching, but the Lord Himself was walking with me, drawing me to Himself as only He can. I still didn't understand many things about Scripture back then, but I did start to understand the power of His life-changing love. When I left Bible school, I knew what it meant to be a Christian and I knew what I had to do to continue living in this new joy and freedom that God had freely granted me after repentance. My turning point came after reading some excellent books by Watchman Nee. He explained the meaning of the cross and that BECAUSE OF THE CROSS, I don't have to strive to be a "good Christian" and make my salvation "stick." Jesus did everything for me already when He died on the cross. He forgave me my sins, past, present and future. He washed me, cleansed me, and secured me for His kingdom, both on this earth and in heaven when I die. Does any of this make sense to us if all we are is religious? No. For only by identifying with the cross of Christ, can we ever begin to know the POWER it has to save us, change us, and lead us to a secure place where we will forever be with the Lord.

Application

Read: 1 Corinthians 1:18-31

Pray: If you are not yet saved, turn to page 61 and make a confession of your faith. If you are saved, pray for those who aren't.

Reflect: How has the cross of Christ affected you in your life? Write about it and prayerfully share your testimony with an unsaved friend.

Day 15 - <u>A Heart Issue</u>

And they rose early in the morning, and went forth into the wilderness of Tekoa: and as they went forth, Jehoshaphat stood and said, Hear me, O Judah, and ye inhabitants of Jerusalem; Believe in the LORD your God, so shall ye be established; believe his prophets, so shall ye prosper.
2 Chronicles 20:20

A guest on a popular Christian TV talk show was discussing the difference between faith and hope. He said that faith is of the heart, and hope is of the mind (See Romans 10:8). We read the Word of God which creates faith in our heart, then we hope for the things we've asked for, with our mind. After hearing this and thinking about it, I believe the Lord gave me even more insight. God puts His desires for us in our heart! So when we feel stirred in our heart to do something in particular, that is God gently directing us what to do.

Many times in my life I have wondered what to do, from which career path to take to where to live. Being a writer, and then later an artist and crafter, I was always drawn to whatever is creative. Many times, this has gone against the grain of what others thought I should have been doing — like working in a normal job making good money. But when I did do what others thought, like work in a good-paying government office job, other than pay my way through university, the job provided no joy or satisfaction whatsoever. I did not want to be there and I did not prosper. There was nothing creative about it!

After marrying my wonderful husband who supports me in all my creative endeavors, I quit my office job and then began doing what was in my heart to do all along — I was able to write full time. This has never been a source of income and neither has my artistic endeavors. This would make me feel bad that I wasn't contributing financially to help pay some bills, or be able to buy extra things that were needed. But my husband, seeing how happy and prosperous I was whenever I created something, insisted that I continue with my writing and artwork. And God would keep stirring me to create more books and more paintings or more new jewelry or sewing creations. Whatever is creative has poured out of me. It seems that the more I create, the more creativity is given to me to keep creating.

Of all the things I have done, I have been given the assurance that in the area of my art, God would prosper me. And the books keep on coming. I finish one and then God inspires me to write another. There are two or three in the waiting almost all the time. Has God laid it on my heart to create? Most definitely. Do I struggle with my thoughts that being creative doesn't really contribute financially in a way that a normal paying job would? I do, almost every day. Yet, the Lord continues to inspire me and I continue to create, loving the beauty of what's created and then seeing the joy it sometimes brings others in seeing my creations. So when God puts a strong desire in your heart to do something, or create something, don't ignore it. It may be a promising future for you, even though others may think it doesn't fit the norm.

Application

Read: Romans 10:8-17

Pray: about your own journey of faith. Ask God to reveal what He has put in your heart to do.

Reflect: Is God stirring you to do something that you have not yet responded to? Respond today and share with someone your new endeavor.

Day 16 - <u>Out of Sight</u>

And he said unto them, Take heed, and beware of covetousness: for a man's life consisteth not in the abundance of the things which he possesseth.
Luke 12:15

As I discussed in the devotional for Day 9, one summer I got rid of many things that we had been storing in our shed at the Beach. Once things were packed away in bags and boxes and left the house to be given to a charity, I really didn't miss anything that we had given. It was as if once it was out of sight, it was also out of mind. These things no longer occupied my space, my thoughts or my life in any way. It wasn't until later that I realized how important a role sight plays in our mind and how what we want and hold onto can really affect our heart. In the opening verse, Jesus is warning us against covetousness. To covet means we have allowed something we want or already have to take hold in our heart. We can become obsessed with things, and this is the danger that Jesus is talking about.

Many years ago, a dear friend of mine came over to my apartment for a visit. We prayed together and the Lord revealed to her that I had a covetous heart. I was quite surprised by this, but later, realized she was right. I was wanting expensive things and also holding onto things not wanting to let go. So I threw away many prized treasures and things of my past (diaries, tapes, some jewelry and other things) that I had been unwillingly to part with. This was not easy, and I grieved for the loss of my diaries since they contained many memories of my childhood. But I knew that because it was in my heart to keep these things and not let go that I was really chained to my past. I had to learn to trust Jesus to restore the memories of my childhood as I needed to remember them, then just let the rest go and trust Him.

Before getting rid of these things, I lived mostly in my

Day 16

past because my past defined who I was at the time. And if I wasn't thinking about my past, I was living in the future, planning and dreaming. I really wasn't enjoying my life in the present and certainly not trusting God as I should have been. Getting rid of those things also encouraged me to learn to live in the present, day by day, enjoying whatever the day offered me. So the day my friend came over and prayed with me was really a great gift from God — I was able to let go of my past and the things that were tying me down, learn to live one day at a time, and learn to trust God unafraid of what the future might hold.

Perhaps not everyone struggles with letting go of their past or even their material things. But covetousness can strike us in different ways at any time. It is wanting anything we can't have or won't let go of, and it is something we hold dearly in our heart. When we read on from Luke 12:15, Jesus gives an interesting story of a rich man who is more concerned about storing his things than he is about the kingdom of God. But rather than being able to enjoy his wealth, he dies that same night. Jesus goes on to say that we should never worry about material things — God will provide it all. So when it comes to what we see and what our heart desires, may we be careful to not allow it to enter our hearts, for once it's lodged there, we run the very real risk of covetousness, and this will add nothing to our lives.

Application

Read: Luke 12:15-31

Pray: Ask God to search your heart for any covetousness. Be willing to hand over to Him anything He finds.

Reflect: Have you ever been asked to let go of something that you treasured? What happened? Journal your thoughts about covetousness as it may relate to you now.

Day 17 - <u>A Way Out</u>

There hath no temptation taken you but such as is common to man: but God is faithful, who will not suffer you to be tempted above that ye are able; but will with the temptation also make a way to escape, that ye may be able to bear it. 1 Corinthians 10:13

Out at the Beach, we have a private back yard, which is fenced in all around and keeps out stray dogs and cats that may wander in. Yet, we still have chipmunks that scurry in and out looking for peanuts or birdseeds. Sometimes they get so familiar with us, they run right in front of us. They have even run across our feet giving us a startle and then a laugh. We were amazed when they'd run right in front of our cat Meesha, tempting fate again and again. In the fall when we'd feed them birdseed, I'd watch them fill their face so full their little cheeks would be bulging out and they'd scurry off to their hide-away where they were storing food for the winter to come. I marveled that God's creatures are so intelligent, preparing for winter and knowing where to find their food, including from humans kind enough to remember them.

One summer, I was working inside going through things that needed to be sorted, discarded or repacked, and a thought came to me that I should go outside. I had no idea why. So I went into the back yard where we have a screened enclosure (the kind that you place on top of a large picnic umbrella and drape around your table). I heard the loudest squeals you can imagine and noticed the screen in disarray. When I got closer, I saw two chipmunks running around and around inside the screen on the ground looking for a way to get out. I quickly lifted the screen and off they went. I wondered how long they had been trapped in there since I couldn't hear them from inside the house. Then I believe that it was God who gave me the thought to go outside even though I didn't know why at the time.

Day 17

Later, I realized how much God cares about His creation and that He oversees everything. If He cared enough about the chipmunks and notified me to go outside to free them, how much more does He care about me and you when we are trapped in some way? I thought about all the situations I've been in where I could not see a way out. Mostly, it has been financial when I was still single and would have car repairs, or the time I couldn't work for over a year. I've struggled with my thoughts and depression and would try everything to find a way out. I would even turn to other religions to see if they had an answer for my negative thinking patterns. After many trials, I would turn to God and He alone would provide my way of escape.

In the opening verse, we are offered great assurance and comfort when it comes to trials. God will only allow what we are able to bear and He will also provide the way of escape. This gives us cause to consider the kind of stress we may be going through even now. Are we being tested as ordained by God, or are we stressed because of our own doing? Either way, He has promised us a way of escape if we but ask, and then we will receive the freedom He offers us today.

Application

Read: 1 Corinthians 10:1-13

Pray: If you feel trapped, ask God to free you, then thank Him for doing so.

Reflect: Have you ever felt trapped and could see no way out? Write about it. Pray for a friend who may feel trapped and encourage them with your own story.

Day 18 - <u>Pool Problems</u>

Trust in the LORD with all thine heart; and lean not unto thine own understanding. In all thy ways acknowledge him, and he shall direct thy paths.
Proverbs 3:5-6

Every summer for about the past five years, we have enjoyed an above ground back yard pool at the lake. It is about 42 inches deep and 15 feet around. In the hot summers, it has provided a welcome retreat and has provided hours of enjoyment and relaxation. The best part is that it's private, well taken care of and convenient. But one spring, my husband felt strongly that we shouldn't put up the pool. For one thing, he felt that the pool itself may have been exposed to the sun for too many years and may no longer be safe. So when we went to the states, we bought another pool for a very reasonable price to replace the one we had. He also discovered that it would need to be placed about 10 feet away from the septic tank. In order to do this, he would need to do extensive landscaping which would include ripping out part of the sidewalk to make sure the ground was level. He was prepared to do all of this.

But July was mostly rainy, so he couldn't start on the landscaping. The last week of July, things started warming up and there was no rain in sight, but by this time, my husband was working a lot of overtime and would not have time to do the landscaping, but he was going to try anyways. So I went to a local lumber yard to buy some supplies and while I was there I mentioned what we were doing. I mentioned how busy we were and a worker offered to assemble a platform for the pool, and then my husband wouldn't have to do the landscaping. He came over the following day and put up the platform. The next day he put up the pool and started filling it with water. But there was a problem — the platform needed a stronger undergirding since it would be holding up tons of water. So we shut off

Day 18

the water and ordered sand to put under the platform. That night we noticed how low the water pressure was. We called a plumber the following morning and he checked things out and informed us that we needed a new well. We phoned the drilling company and were told that it would be close to $6,000. Now we know why my husband felt he shouldn't put the pool up in the first place! We decided to wait on the well until spring, took the pool down and then stored it. Every door had been closed in regards to putting up the pool.

In the meantime, our new neighbour offered to hook up our hose to his well, so we could continue to come out and have the use of water. We lent him and his family our unused freezer that they needed. This began to create a friendly and trusting relationship with our neighbours. My husband's father was ill and needed extra care, so rather than stay out at the Beach, we moved back to our condo in the city to be available to him. Meanwhile, I was missing the Beach and the pool that never did go up. Instead, I used the pool at the condo. Every hot day, I'd go out to the pool and God had a special treat in store for me — new friends that also enjoyed swimming. Rather than be by myself at the Beach, now I had the benefit of a pool that was well cared for and new friends that I enjoyed being with. Sometimes things don't always turn out the way we want, but God has something better in store. May we always trust Him that He knows what's best, and follow the direction He gives.

Application

Read: Romans 8:28-32

Pray: for a situation in your life that you are struggling with. Ask for God's leading and then do what He asks you to do.

Reflect: Has God ever closed a door that you wanted left open? What happened? Share your experience with a friend.

Day 19 - <u>A New View</u>

While we look not at the things which are seen, but at the things which are not seen: for the things which are seen are temporal; but the things which are not seen are eternal. 2 Corinthians 4:18

Sometimes a new thing can open up a whole new world for us and can make a big difference in our lives. For instance, our neighbours came home one afternoon towing a motor boat behind their van. Now rather than just view the lake from the shore, they would be traveling on the lake noticing the shore! Their world is expanded to include wherever water can take you. They will visit marinas, lakes, creeks and so on and can go anywhere with their motor boat. We experienced this to some degree when we bought our canoe.

When we bought our camper, we started discovering campgrounds that provided a new view. This jolted us out of our comfort zone, especially when we camped in or near wooded areas where bears live. Rather than have breakfast in our kitchen at home, we'd enjoy our toast and eggs on a rocky ledge overlooking a serene lake in northern Ontario. When we weren't camping, we'd take trips by car or van and have whatever views the hotels offered. The best view we had was when we stayed in a posh hotel in Florida. Our balcony overlooked the Gulf of Mexico. Every night we would see a lone white crane slowly strutting along the shores, a scene that I remember well to this day.

Almost everyone I know likes traveling in some form because it offers a different view of things. Not only do we see new and different things, it can also change our perspective on things. We may be burdened down with our jobs, or find ourselves bogged down in the daily grind of just living, so find that a vacation is just what the doctor ordered. But vacations only provide temporary relief, because we always must come home to face the same

Day 19

problems all over again. Even boating has special challenges, like making sure you have enough gas, and being careful around other boaters, not to mention sudden storms that can come upon you. And anyone who has ever camped can relate to a different kind of stress since you are literally re-creating your home in small quarters and putting up with all kinds of weather and unwanted bugs. So what is the answer?

In the opening verse, we are offered a new and radical way of viewing things. Rather than look at the things the world and even nature has to offer, we are to look beyond this. Our focus is not to be on the things of this world because those things are temporary. God knows that we need something much deeper than what we see on the surface. We need to see things through spiritual eyes; these are the eternal things that God presents to us. What might these things be? They are when your neighbour has a need that you can fulfill. They are when the pastor of your church needs you to lead the song service. They are when your friend calls at an inconvenient time because they need to talk. Eternal things are the deeds waiting to be fulfilled through us, the unseen things that are the most important to God.

Application

Read: 2 Corinthians 4:15-18

Pray: Ask God to reveal eternal things to you and to help you make these a priority rather than temporal things.

Reflect: What are some unseen eternal things God has revealed to you? What will you do to fulfill unseen things so that God is glorified and others are encouraged?

Day 20 - <u>Beware the Senses</u>

But we have this treasure in earthen vessels, that the excellency of the power may be of God, and not of us. 2 Corinthians 4:7

One summer day I was sitting in the car dealership waiting for my car to have the oil changed. I started reading an article in a popular magazine that grabbed my attention. It was about a man that had severe emotional problems and was thinking of ending his life. In so many words, he recognized that there was a voice talking to him that he didn't recognize as his own. He couldn't identify the source, but it was enough to make him stop what he was contemplating and research further into this strange and interesting phenomenon. Also, he realized that the real person inside would never do such a thing as end his own life, and that by listening to this deceptive voice, he was more like a slave to the voice than the master of his own identity. Basically, the negative voice held him captive, making him feel trapped and enslaved.

I found this quite fascinating and wanted to go home and pray about what I had read, to see what the Lord would teach me about it. The Lord didn't answer me right away, but wanted me to wait. That evening I shared what I had read with some Christian friends. Clearly, the man that had written the article used terms common to those of a Buddhist persuasion. Our group had some interesting insights, but nothing, I felt, that really answered the questions I had about what I had read. It would take some more study and prayer. The next day I was listening to Christian TV programs and it was then that the Lord clearly spoke to me about what I had read. One pastor spoke about "authority" (who is in authority over our lives). Another pastor spoke about I Peter 1:18-19, that we are bought with a price and belong to Christ. Then I received a very clear instruction to go into my quiet room and God was going to give me an outline for a new book about the soul. One of the chapter headings is about authority. The title is "Under Whose Authority?" It was here that I received my answer.

The author who had shared his story and how he discovered that another voice was feeding him negative and destructive information, was under the authority of what I now believe was Satan's voice. When a person leaves their mind open and it is not under the authority of the Holy Spirit (or Jesus), many negative thoughts will try to invade and control our thinking. When I am under the trusting and loving authority of Jesus, the battle is given over completely to Him. Truly, we are victorious even when we feel down, depressed or hear negative news. In the opening verse, we can picture a fragile vase that has been molded on the kiln by a Master Artist. Inside the vase, He has poured His Spirit, a power so much greater than anything we can think or imagine, and one we can use at just a mere whisper of His name. Many things may happen to the vessel, but the power within will not be affected. Are we beset by many thoughts that threaten to destroy us? We already know the source is Satan. May we boldly proclaim our victory and remember to use the power of God freely given to every believer.

Application

<u>Read</u>: 2 Corinthians 4:6-12

<u>Pray</u>: If you are struggling with negative thoughts, give them over to Jesus and thank Him for the victory that is yours today.

<u>Reflect</u>: How have you handled negative thoughts, or helped others who have struggled this way? Help someone today who is struggling with negative thinking.

Day 21 - <u>Prepare for Battle</u>

For if the trumpet give an uncertain sound, who shall prepare himself to the battle?
1 Corinthians 14:8

One day I was reading the above passage of Scripture and realized that everything God does is with a distinct purpose and is backed by an impeccable sense of order. Just look at the universe, the stars and especially the many wonders of nature. Nothing is amiss or out of place. If we are to look at the whole idea of a battle, we might think of various wars going on in our world right now. Imagine how chaotic these wars would be if Generals or heads of the war departments did not have a battle plan or a strategy. Not only would they lose their own battle, but the war would truly be fought in vain with no wins, but only senseless losses.

Similarly, in our daily lives, as Christians, we are in a different kind of battle, mostly with our thoughts. We might have a very busy life and go through many battles even in a single day. My battles in the mind usually begin as I wake up, and it's not until I start to pray or read God's Word that my thoughts begin to line up with Scripture, and then I become prepared for the day. One day I had a particularly difficult day. Following a yearly doctor's visit, I had to go for a few routine tests. On the way home, another driver was extremely annoyed with me when he felt I cut him off, even though I didn't think I did. Then when I got home I had to set up yet another appointment for another medical test. Then the phone rang and it was the dental office telling me they had a cancellation and could I come in in two days to complete some dental work? The following day I was to go to our Beach house and finish painting part of the inside of the house. My husband and I had spent the past 10 days or so painting all the ceilings, a complete large office and then the main large living room area, and were still trying to recuperate from all the hard work we had done. Also that same week I was to take a three hour drive to the small town where my mom lives and also where my sister would be visiting. Then I'd be driving them both back to the city with me for the weekend and they'd be staying with me, something I was really looking forward to. But talk about busyness and stress!

In the midst of all these events, I cried out to God with a simple "Help!" and then He directed me to the opening verse. I thought about all the events crowding into my week, making me feel a sense of panic and wondering if I could accomplish it all without having a nervous breakdown. Then I thought about what I was thinking about — were my thoughts peaceful, ordered and full of good fruits, or were they harried, anxious and worrisome? I had to confess that they were the latter. Then I prayed and the Lord helped me believe in the positive and switch my thoughts to positive ones. I was directed to focus on the moment, not the next hour and not the next day, certainly not the whole week as it lay ahead of me. I was to trust Him for the moment only. Tomorrow He would take care of me then. Do your thoughts have an uncertain sound, or are they a clear directive from the Lord, filling you with purpose and peace? May we quiet ourselves enough to hear and recognize His voice.

Application

Read: James 3:17-18

Pray: Ask God to help order your thoughts and remove any thoughts not from Him. Pray for His peace to fill you.

Reflect: Do you have any areas in your life that fill you with uncertainty? Bring them to the Lord, then share your victory with a friend.

Day 22 – <u>A Comforting Shelter</u>

He that dwelleth in the secret place of the most High shall abide under the shadow of the Almighty. Psalm 91:1

When my sister and I were kids, our family lived a little on the outskirts of town. We had a big yard and lots of bushes and trees especially on the west side of the property, which gave us lots of neat places to hide. Along with the neighbour kids, one time we thought it might be fun to build a fort or a clubhouse in the wooded bushes. So we found some spare lumber, used twigs and branches and whatever else we could find and made a make-shift fort, hidden from view by most adults. Rain or shine, we used our little shelter and held meetings there, deciding what we would do from time to time to have fun. We not only had a fort, but sometimes we'd get to sleep in my brother's tent in the back yard when he wasn't using it. How thrilling to sleep outside in the comfort of a cozy tent! We also made a cozy little get-away in our narrow attic in the house upstairs. We had a blanket, candles and would sometimes read in there. It seemed we were always discovering or creating little hideaways when we were kids. One time we made a little house out of the huge box the new freezer came in, but it didn't last long because there was no place to keep such a large box! In the winter, we made forts in the high snow banks in the back yard.

Years later when my husband and I adopted two cats, we noticed that the small pure black one, Espresso, liked to hide under the blankets on the bed. We'd call him and be looking for him for the longest time. Finally, we noticed an unusual lump on the bed and would find him snuggled there as cozy, warm and contented as can be. We also bought them two kitty bassinets which they climb into every so often, snuggle in and then sleep contentedly. There's something about having a shelter that brings us a sense of well-being, safety

Day 22

and security. When we feel this way, we are better able to rest and relax. Yet, even with a safe and cozy place to be, many things in life can happen to upset our sense of security and well-being. Because we live in a fallen world, things are not perfect. People may say or do things to hurt us. We can lose a job or our health. The things we run to for shelter and comfort can be taken away or we can feel threatened that we will lose what peace and security we have.

Not too long ago, I was doing a lot of writing, intent on completing the books as the Lord kept inspiring me to write. I was feeling overwhelmed and a little sad and didn't know why. I asked the Lord about it and He said I was under attack from the enemy because of writing the books. So I prayed that He would hide me under the shadow of His wing out of sight from the enemy's radar, and also to take away the cloud of oppression if it wasn't sent from Him. I noticed an immediate release from the gloominess I was feeling and I began to picture myself hiding under the shadow of the Lord's wings. What an amazingly safe place to be — there is no place safer! So whenever you feel you need shelter from feeling threatened, afraid or anxious, run into the safe loving shelter of the Lord — He'll always welcome you.

Application

Read: Psalm 91

Pray: for God to show you His safe place if you feel anxious or afraid. Thank Him for His provision of safety for you.

Reflect: What is your idea of a safe place? Write about it and then journal your thoughts about Psalm 91

Day 23 - <u>Attracted to the Light</u>

Let your light so shine before men, that they may see your good works, and glorify your Father which is in heaven. Matthew 5:16

One warm summer night, my husband and I were working outside taking screws out of a platform that we were going to use to hold a pool. As the sunlight faded and darkness fell upon us, we used a trouble light and flashlights so that we could better see what we were doing. The bugs were numerous and kept swarming around us, but as soon as they noticed the light coming from the lamp, they flew into the light. I said to my husband, "Now the bugs are more attracted to the light than they are to me." As I thought about this statement, a profound idea struck me. As Christians, I wondered, Do we try to attract attention to ourselves thinking this will bring the lost to Christ, or do we rely on the light of the Holy Spirit within us to do a much better job?

About a month later, I was back at the Beach working hard painting the inside of the house. One morning I woke up and the Lord was directing me to read Matthew 5. My eyes fell on the above verse. Once again, I had been so focused on my many tasks at hand, that I was forgetting about being with others. I knew that the Lord wanted me to go out and be with people. Later that morning the phone rang and it was my friend inviting me to join her and another friend for lunch at a local restaurant. Of course I jumped at the chance. What does it mean to let our light shine? I believe it means that we embrace the Father's heart to love people and care about them, to be available to people and to be willing to offer a kind word, a kind deed and some means of fellowship. Of course, there are no limits to what we can do to make someone's day a brighter one.

When I went for lunch with my two friends, the waitress

seemed to be so serious and quiet — I thought she might be having a bad day. Being a waitress is no easy task, with people wanting their coffee right away, and serving several tables all at once. I know because I've been there. When I went to pay for my meal, I thanked her and she smiled for the first time and called me "dear." Was this the Lord showing me that the light in me was shining and the waitress had needed a simple kind word? Too often, we become judgmental and avoid people we think are unfriendly, or we become too practical and perhaps think that going out to a restaurant is expensive and not the place to minister to people. Or we become too religious and high-minded, thinking that ministry is a neat and tidy business. So we put off ministry waiting for the perfect time when people will be open and willing to listen to what we have to say. Perhaps we are setting our sights too high, when all the Lord has asked us to do is to go out and mingle with people, like Jesus did in His earthly ministry. You'll note that when you read the New Testament, the people Jesus ministered to were found in the most unlikely places — at a well, in restaurants where people drank alcohol, on the streets, at fisherman's wharfs, in the marketplaces, and interestingly, rarely in the synagogue. May we be open to the simplest form of ministry and know that it is most profound when the Lord is shining through us.

Application

Read: Matthew 5:14-16

Pray: for God to show you where He wants you to minster. Pray for those He will send your way.

Reflect: What have been your most meaningful experiences in ministering to people? What happened? Make a plan to go out today to minster to someone in some way.

Day 24 - <u>Circle of Intimacy</u>

Henceforth I call you not servants; for the servant knoweth not what his lord doeth: but I have called you friends; for all things that I have heard of my Father I have made known unto you. John 15:15

One late evening I was watching TV and a Christian counselor for married couples was on a call-in talk show. A lady called in and said that her in-laws were not treating her very well and it was becoming increasingly difficult for her to be with them. The counselor advised that in every family there is a circle of intimacy. When a person in that circle is mistreated, they must step back a notch and leave that circle of intimacy even for a time until the situation can be resolved. After all, intimacy is built on love and trust and if those things are violated, it is no longer an intimate relationship, but one that is bordering on abusive. The counselor had excellent advise to this wife. He said that her husband should continue to see his family, but that she should not until he could talk to his parents and explain how his wife was feeling. When his parents were willing and able to make her feel welcome again and treat her with respect, then she could return to that circle of intimacy.

After watching this program, I started thinking about intimacy in relationships. As a Christian, I have always found it best to keep short accounts with loved ones and friends. It is not always easy to love and forgive when someone is saying hurting things to us or about us. If only we knew the burdens each other is carrying, I am sure we would think twice before adding more insult upon injury. In-law troubles are especially inevitable, since each partner wants to please each separate family. How important open discussion is in all of our relationships, especially with our closest family and friends!

Day 24

I believe the Lord gave us an amazing example of what it means to have intimate friends when He chose His twelve disciples. Jesus was and is the King of Kings and Lord of Lords, and all of us are subject to His authority and power, whether we know Him or not. Yet in the opening verse, rather than consider His disciples servants, He called them "friends." Then He explains what that friendship is based on — COMMUNICATION! He said that whatever His Father said to Him, He shared with them. That is true friendship — sharing and caring. What does this say about not communicating and remaining silent? It means that either we don't care to share ourselves with others, or we are too afraid to say something in case we are judged for what we say. Or perhaps it means we are angry or bitter and have vowed not to trust anyone. Maybe we are just too tired and can't be bothered to work at relationships. This is the surest way to cut ourselves and others off from intimacy, since intimacy is not possible without some kind of positive communication. But, there is a great added bonus to intimacy amongst family and friends — it takes away our loneliness and it also sets an incredible example to the rest of the world who will be so impressed they will want to be drawn into our warm circle of intimacy.

Application

<u>Read</u>:   John 15:13-16

<u>Pray</u>: Ask God to reveal any areas of hurt that need healing. Ask Him for forgiveness and restoration with Him and others.

<u>Reflect</u>: What are your most intimate relationships? In what ways can they be improved? Begin improving them today.

Day 25 - <u>What's in a Name?</u>

For I am not ashamed of the gospel of Christ: for it is the power of God unto salvation to every one that believeth; to the Jew first, and also to the Greek.
Romans 1:16

When I was a teenager I had a life-changing experience that took place in a small Bible school in Saskatchewan. It was here that I was delivered from a sinful life that was killing me, and instead, discovered the love and grace of God. I will never forget this experience, since it changed my life forever and then led me on to a ministry that has also changed other people's lives. This transformation created such a zeal in me to spread the good news of the power and love of Jesus, that I witnessed to many people, not caring if they labeled me "fanatical" or worse.

Not too long ago I learned about a Bible college that decided to become accredited and become more of a university than a Bible college. As part of this change, they decided to drop the word "Bible" from their name since some students did not want the name "Bible" listed on their resume as part of their academic credentials. As a Christian, this news greatly surprised me. The college was trying to fulfill its mission to train up missionaries. Yet, at the same time they were trying to reach academic standards that would please the students, and also enable their resumes to appear more sophisticated and up to date even to other Christian mission organizations around the globe! I wondered if we have become altogether too "politically correct" to the extent that it even affects our testimony of the Gospel message.

After my one year at Bible school, I remember applying for jobs. If I was ashamed that the word "Bible" appeared on my resume, then would I also be ashamed to call myself a Christian? For many years, I was proud to list the name of

Day 25

the Bible college I had attended on my resume, and it even opened up opportunities for me to not only witness to the people who were interviewing me for a job, but also got me hired when the interviewer discovered I was a Christian. It worked in my favor since the employer, seeing that I went to a "Bible" college, felt that I could be trusted and that I would likely be a good worker!

Furthermore, as a high school teacher, I enjoy working with teenagers and seeing them mature and come into their own. But I also see a lack of proper guidance in the schools and now even in the Bible colleges and other educational organizations. As a child, I remember looking up to adults, teachers, Sunday School teachers and anyone else entrusted with teaching me, especially when it came to spiritual truths. This provided a moral and upright grounding for me later on right up to this day. One of the things I was taught was to stand up and not be afraid to share my faith. I was also warned that if I am ashamed of Jesus before man, He will be ashamed of me when He returns (see Mark 8:38). It's a sobering thought to consider what God's opinion of us is when we start eliminating important words like the "Bible," from our resumes of life. May we seek to please Him in all ways, remembering, that one day we will give an account and either will stand before Him ashamed or will be rewarded for our sacrifices of putting self and our pride aside.

Application

Read: Galatians 1:6-12

Pray: Ask God to help you in any area where you might struggle to lift up Jesus Name and be a witness for Him.

Reflect: Have you ever suffered because you are a Christian? What happened? Do something today for the sake of the Lord that may cost you something.

Day 26 - <u>Short-change Religion</u>

Jesus saith unto him, I am the way, the truth, and the life: no man cometh unto the Father, but by me.
John 14:6

One day I received a call from an acquaintance I had met through my writing courses that I offered. We always seemed to get into the most interesting topics. He explained that his dad taught him that religions mean all the same thing, but people have a different name for God. Although I didn't want to get into any deep theological debate with him, I did share my testimony that there is only One person who can set us truly free and that is Jesus Christ. He is the only One who died for our sins and then miraculously rose again. In fact, even His birth was miraculous. His entire life was based on miracles and He still performs miracles every single day, so many in fact, they would likely outnumber the sand on the seashore stretched from one end of the earth to the other. He is a great and mighty God.

For people growing up in non-Christian cultures, like my friend was, they would think that we have a carte blanche when it comes to what we want to believe. We can choose any religion and that it's perfectly alright. Although this may be true, there is still the matter of eternity — no religion on this earth can get us into heaven. Jesus made this very clear in the opening passage of Scripture. I have talked to other friends who believe that everyone is good and has a piece of God within them. They believe that people are only bad because they are taught to be bad. If they are shown how to be good, they will be good people. Yet, history records, that some of the most notorious criminals came from a good and cultured background. For example, some of the terrorist groups of the 60s era came from wealthy and well-known families in the United States and parts of Europe. And all you have to do is look at a baby, crying and demanding attention, then when it can talk, quickly learning to say no.

Day 26

Where do they learn this? In school, whenever I have taught children of any age, there is usually one or two students that demand my attention. They will do this by acting out and causing a constant disruption until they are gently, but firmly disciplined and asked to behave or leave the class. Some will try your patience to the very limit. Other children are compliant and easy to teach.

Yet no matter how "good" or "bad" a person is, the Bible records that man is born sinful and this is all he knows how to do until he meets Jesus and discovers the depth of his own inability to overcome sin and how sinful he really is. Religion only masks the problem, since going to church and being nice to people cannot begin to change a sinful heart. Only Jesus can do that. I have heard testimony after testimony of God's saving grace and the many miracles He can and will perform. Once a heart has been touched and changed by Jesus, every other religion in the world pales to what He can do and to Who He is. No one would want to turn to an empty religion after they have met Jesus. This is guaranteed, if only people would give Him a chance. May we be always Christ-like, but never religious, for religion is the surest path to a godless hell with no hope of redemption.

Application

<u>Read</u>: John 14:1-6

<u>Pray</u>: for those you know who are religious, but spiritually lost. Ask God to use you to reach them.

<u>Reflect</u>: Have you ever been religious, but not Christ-like? Journal your thoughts on how you would like to be more Christ-like. Share your testimony with a religious but unsaved friend, and then invite them to your church.

Day 27 - <u>Summer Olympics</u>

Know ye not that they which run in a race run all, but one receiveth the prize? So run, that ye may obtain. 1 Corinthians 9:24

In the summer of 2008, the world saw some of the most magnificent displays celebrating and surrounding the Olympics in Beijing, China. I caught glimpses of it whenever I had the chance, and one evening I watched the girl's beach volleyball. Each team of two girls (one from the US and the other from China) were a good match, but clearly the US kept one point ahead throughout the match. One of the US players had participated in the Olympics for many years and had learned a sure-winning strategy that would win her the gold medal almost every time. She would hit the ball over the net and it would make a dive to the ground so fast, the opposing team members never had a chance to catch it and tether it back. She won by experience and strategy.

I also watched women's diving. We were astounded when a small 15 year old girl from China won. It was also interesting and sad to watch a US diver make her last dive since she was retiring after several years of participating in the Olympics. Later, she responded to the interviewer with tears, and she also hugged her coach as a last goodbye. It is well known that participating in sports such as Olympic training will eventually take a toll on a person's body and retirement is inevitable as a person ages. But I had to admire these champions, for whether they won or lost, the effort they put in to qualify for the Olympics and to win is more than most of us probably do in a lifetime.

As Christians, we are also in a race to win, far more important than any Olympic game, that will come and be quickly gone. In thinking about my own race to win, it has always been to write and FINISH my books. For many years, I lived an undisciplined life, dreaming about being a writer,

Day 27

but not settling down long enough to actually complete a writing project. After awhile, the dream of doing something becomes a burden and not a joy because it is pressing on you to at least begin the project. In thinking about the single-minded focus that an Olympian must have to succeed, I can also relate to the importance of this in my own life experience. Many things will come and distract me from the task of writing. Almost every day when I sit down to write, the phone will ring. Usually it's an unsolicited call from a company wanting me to buy something. Or suddenly my life will fill up with things that need my immediate attention. Sometimes it's the cats needing to be fed or I need to clean up a spill somewhere.

But like the girls volleyball player from the US, I have learned an effective strategy to win and get the job done. When I know I am going to write, I pray and ask God to help me focus, give me His thoughts and guide me throughout the process. Really, it is so simple — Jesus must be invited into the process. He has never failed to be with me and guide me and inspire me. How exciting when you think about it. He doesn't ask us to run a race without first equipping us. And He does not abandon us once we set out to win. He wants us to succeed in everything we do. Like anyone wanting to win, all we have to do is begin and then believe we will finish the course when the Lord is our Trainer and Coach.

Application

<u>Read</u>: 1 Corinthians 9:24-27

<u>Pray</u>: Ask God to help you begin and complete any projects He has laid on your heart to do.

<u>Reflect</u>: Write about your greatest accomplishment and what you did to succeed at it. Begin another task today that the Lord has laid on your heart to do.

Day 28 - <u>Atmosphere of Praise</u>

Praise ye the LORD: for it is good to sing praises unto our God; for it is pleasant; and praise is comely. Psalm 147:1

I mentioned earlier that I went to Bible school and a great transformation took place in my heart and in my life. During this time, when I first arrived and for a couple months afterward, I still did not understand the marvelous ways of God and I didn't know about the love of God yet. I had come from a hippy culture where rock and roll music was a big part of it, along with the mood-altering drugs. Drugs have a hypnotic effect and give the illusion of the supernatural, because they distort your senses and you start to see things and hear things that don't exist in the natural world. In a real sense, a person under the influence of drugs, no longer has control over their thoughts or actions, depending of course, on the kind of and amount of drugs that have been taken. This is where Satan comes in and plays havoc with people's minds.

In my case, my bout with this drug-induced life ended in a nervous breakdown. Strangely, I found solace in the rock and roll, heavy metal music I listened to even after I enrolled in Bible school. But this gradually began to change as other students introduced me to a new kind of music — Christian contemporary. There was one group I was particularly drawn to, whose music was Scripture-based and extremely worshipful to God called, *The Second Chapter of Acts*. For years I listened to their music and to this very day, listen to them. Music was also important to me because my career had been and would be Entertainment Editor of newspapers. I had been to many concerts in the city, had sometimes interviewed the musicians and would continue to do so later in the Christian world. So for a good part of my life I have followed the trends of music and listened to the various groups that have sprung up through the years.

Day 28

In the last ten years or so, I noticed a new trend in the Christian world — a lot of the music is based on personal feelings and experiences and fails to lift up God in a way that truly praises Him. What is praiseworthy music? In Bible school, we had early morning chapel each day before attending classes. This was strictly a time of praise and worship, prayer requests, and a short sermonette. I can tell you that many times we never got to the prayer requests and the sermonette. The time of singing and praise would last for hours, and some days we wouldn't get to class until the afternoon. How can this be? When we started to praise and worship, this invited the presence of God into the room (a warmth and power so great it went beyond your natural senses). In the presence of God, many miracles began to happen (some seen, many unseen). We were in awe at the power and presence of God where there is a gentle peace, no sense of time, and no fear. People were healed inside and out, many were empowered with the gift of tongues followed by the interpretation, and everyone was encouraged and in some way changed by being in His presence. This is a far cry from the pathetic temporary high that drugs offered. Our lives were forever changed that year and we learned something about praise. Nothing is more powerful than praise and will invite God's presence into your life almost instantaneously. Try it today and see what happens!

Application

Read: Psalm 150

Pray: Spend time in praise and thankfulness.

Reflect: Think of a time or times when you praised God. What happened? Praise Him today and every day.

Day 29 - <u>Rulership</u>

And God said, Let us make man in our image, after our likeness: and let them have dominion over the fish of the sea, and over the fowl of the air, and over the cattle, and over all the earth, and over every creeping thing that creepeth upon the earth.
Genesis 1:26

I once heard a special speaker on a Christian TV show explain the above verse in a way that I had never heard before. He said that when God gave man dominion, this means He gave him rulership that would, of course, be based on a servant heart. Rulership was never meant to harm nature or others, other than what was ordained and okayed by God for His own purposes. This rulership God gave man is based on a covenant relationship. This means that it was entrusted to man to carry out God's best will, and wasn't meant as a selfish means to rule over people in any way that is evil or harmful. We must be thankful for countries that fight for and encourage people's freedoms and frown upon dictatorships.

The speaker also talked about preaching the Gospel and that when we do so, this is taking rulership over what God has done and what He has provided, namely salvation through His Son, Jesus Christ. Many times we may feel intimidated to preach the Gospel, since our culture and society is based on tolerance of every religion and plural belief systems. So this means that if someone wants to believe in any other god rather than the God of the Bible, that they have the right to do so without prejudice or harassment. Yet, if we have God's love in our heart, we will want to reach as many as possible with His life-saving Gospel.

If you think about the concept of rulership, and remember that Satan appeared as a serpent during the time of creation, it is important to note that man was given

Day 29

dominion BEFORE the serpent is even mentioned. The serpent isn't mentioned until Genesis 3:1 when he approaches Eve with his insidious lie. Scholars have noted that since Adam had already been given dominion over the earth, he should have recognized the serpent and driven him from the garden before the inestimable damage was done when they disobeyed God and sinned. So today, although we know the serpent is still roaming about the earth seeking whom he may devour (see I Peter 5:8), we need to remember that we still have rulership over the earth and especially, over Satan and his demons. Satan will try everything in his power to convince us that we do not have rulership, but that he does, so that we will be afraid, uninvolved and do nothing. One of the greatest weapons he uses is the media to broadcast negative news, so that we will be afraid, discouraged and want to hide away or just give up altogether without even trying to establish God's righteousness through concerted prayer and divine instruction. We must never allow negative thoughts to dissuade us, for this is what Satan hopes we will do, which gives him ground to usurp the authority that has been given to us. What is our best defense against such a tricky foe? We must USE the rulership we have been given and stand our ground, which means we take rulership of the WHOLE EARTH as is rightfully ours by God. We do this by prayer and steadfastness, unwavering in our responsibility to govern the whole earth according to the ability and the promises God has given us.

Application

Read: Genesis 1:26-31

Pray: Ask God to help you take rulership over the area where you live and work. Do what He instructs you in that regard.

Reflect: What will you do to take rulership based on a servant heart? Begin today.

Day 30 - <u>So Many Choices</u>

I call heaven and earth to record this day against you, that I have set before you life and death, blessing and cursing: therefore choose life, that both thou and thy seed may live:
Deuteronomy 30:19

For a few years, I knew that I wanted to paint the inside of our house at the Beach. The walls had a wood-look wall board, and I thought it would be a good thing to change the colors to brighten up the living room and office. So a couple of years ago, I bought a can of light yellow paint and a tan color for the trim. Meanwhile we moved to the city and the painting job remained undone. Finally, one late summer, I painted the ceilings and decided it was time to paint the large living room and office. Choosing paint colors is very stressful to me because you really don't know what you're getting and what will be the results until you've painted the entire room. Then when you get different kinds of light, it will appear slightly different in color, whether it be natural sunlight, tungsten light or fluorescent. The color of the floors will also affect the over-all look of the walls. I tried the yellow paint and didn't like it, so I prayed about it and then went and bought a linen-white for the walls and a slightly beige tinge for the trim. I would use the yellow paint later on for the inside of the walk-in closet.

So the problem of which color to choose was solved. But there were more choices once I reached the hardware store. Did I want eggshell, velvet, or semi-gloss? I had no idea. So the clerk suggested velvet for the trim and eggshell for the walls. Then I had to choose brushes, rollers and the size of the paint tray. Then when I went to pay, I had to decide HOW I would pay — cash, which credit card, or debit card? I also had to remember to give them my Aeroplan card so I could get points. Talk about stress! Similarly, when eating out, choosing from a detailed menu is also stressful.

Day 30

First, you have to decide which restaurant to choose, and then what you'll eat and drink, how much to tip, and again, how to pay. These things take time and careful consideration, like so many things in life.

But, does it really matter what paint color we choose or what food to order in a restaurant? No, not in the whole scheme of things. Interestingly, when I looked up the word "choose" in the Bible concordance, I found it mentioned 58 times in the KJV. As I perused the verses, I found that the word is used many more times from God's directive than God saying, "You choose." It was used more as a command of God than man's rightful will to choose. And the context in which it was used had to do with important and strategic commands that would always give Israel an advantage over their enemy, or He meant it as a blessing or some other good. Sometimes I think we place far too much emphasis on our so called "rights," and fail to understand the meaning of free will, which is always with the purpose to glorify God in some way. In the opening verse, God gives one of the most important directives ever — choose life that you may live!

Throughout our time on earth, we will be bombarded with choices of every kind and we will think that these are important — but truly, nothing is more important than choosing Jesus, for without Him, we do not and will not have life. May we choose Him today and experience all the blessings He has in store for us.

Application

Read: Deuteronomy 30:15-20

Pray: For God's will in important matters where you must make a decision.

Reflect: What is the most important choice you ever made? What might be a future one?

An Invitation for Salvation

Dear Friend,

However, this book got into your hands, I hope it has encouraged you. Daily devotions only truly benefit us once we've given our heart and entire life over to the Lord Jesus Christ. If you would like to receive Jesus into your heart and life today and also have the assurance that you will spend eternity in heaven with Him, please begin by saying this prayer:

Dear Heavenly Father,

I come to you in the name of Jesus. Your Word says, "Whosoever shall call upon the name of the Lord shall be saved" (Acts 2:21). I call on you now and ask Jesus to come into my heart, forgive me for all my sins, and cleanse me. I ask you to be Lord over my life according to Romans 10:9-10 — "That if thou shalt confess with thy mouth the Lord Jesus, and shalt believe in thine heart that God hath raised him from the dead, thou shalt be saved. For with the heart man believeth unto righteousness; and with the mouth confession is made unto salvation." I do this now — I confess that Jesus is Lord and I believe in my heart that God raised Him from the dead.

In Jesus Name,
Amen

You are now reborn! You are a Christian and a child of God! Be assured, you have taken the most important step of your life and God has reserved your place in heaven. He will always be with you and lead you into all truth (Hebrews 13:5b; John 14:26). You will need to read the Bible on a daily basis to get to know Him and all the many promises He has for you. As well, don't delay in contacting a Bible-believing church where you will find fellowship with others who have also taken this important life-changing step. May God bless you as you continue on your new path of life and freedom in Christ!

About the Author

Linda McBurney-Gunhouse enjoys her life in Manitoba, Canada. She writes to help others and inspire them to overcome difficulties and achieve success in life. She also enjoys story-telling in the form of writing fiction. Linda has spent a life-time writing and honing her skills. She studied Journalism, English, and History and received both a BA and B.Ed. in English. She has a diploma in magazine writing. She has worked as a contributing editor for a community college and also as an editor for a community newspaper in Winnipeg. Her articles have appeared in national, city and community newspapers and one magazine. She has written and sold one radio play. She is an accomplished eBook author of several inspirational books, including five full-length fiction. Her readership is international, and some of her eBooks frequently reach the Top 100 in specific categories. Linda also writes thought-provoking blogs.

She loves to share her faith and how she has overcome the many challenges in life in a way that readers can relate to. She sometimes teaches Creative Writing, and she does special speaking. She sometimes does free-lance writing for the local newspapers. She has also facilitated her own writer's group in a local setting. She continues to expand her thought-provoking blogs and book-writing. When she is not writing, she loves to be involved in creating several mediums of art.

Other Titles by Linda McBurney-Gunhouse

Inspirational Books

Cures for Stress
Essential Steps to Increase Your Faith
Footpath to Freedom
Freedom Through Spiritual Discernment
Healing & Hope for Child Loss
Healing For The Wounded Soul
Loneliness: The Pathway to Discovery
Making Sense of the Rapture
Money: Master or Servant?
No Fear of Hell
Power Thoughts for Positive Thinking
Spiritual Leadership in a Fallen World
The Act of Decision-Making
The Bible: Conformed or Transformed?
The Journey of Oneness
The Journey to Contentment
The Power of Submission
Victory Over Backsliding
When Love Is All There Is

Biography

The Bonk Saga: A History of Memories
Called to Overcome

Other Titles

Devotionals

Pathways to Devotion I
Pathways to Devotion II
Pathways to Devotion III
Pathways to Devotion IV
Pathways to Devotion V
Pathways to Devotion VI
Pathways to Devotion VII
Pathways to Devotion VIII
Pathways to Devotion IX
Pathways to Devotion X
Pathways to Devotion XI

Fiction

The Redemption of Steep Rock Cove
Return to Steep Rock Cove
Christmas Comes to Steep Rock Cove
Waves of Change at Steep Rock Cove
Driving with the Top Down
Track Three

Poetry Books

Heart Songs
Songs in the Desert
Water Crossings
Wings I: Morning Arising
Wings II: Daylight Reflections
Wings III: Contemplation

Other Titles

Creative How-to Books

Artistic Ideas & Inspirations
How to Create Stories From Your Own Life
Living a Creative Life

Writing Manuals

Creative Writing
Write Your Life Story
Fiction Writing

Please visit our website at www.creativefocus.ca to discover the many books from this list that are available as eBooks.

Note: If you have enjoyed reading this book, or any other eBook of mine, please rate it online, or recommend it on your Facebook page. It will help spread the word, and let others know it is available. My goal is to help, encourage and inspire others through my writing. Thank you and may God richly bless you!

www.ingramcontent.com/pod-product-compliance
Lightning Source LLC
Chambersburg PA
CBHW061342040426
42444CB00011B/3038